The English Grammar Workbook
for Grades 6, 7, and 8

200+ Simple Exercises to Improve Grammar, Punctuation, and Word Usage

TABLE OF CONTENTS

THE FOUR TYPES OF SENTENCES

A. Circle declarative, interrogative, exclamatory, or imperative to describe each sentence.

1. Never take chances on a climb.   *interrogative*   *imperative*

2. It is crucial to take care of your equipment.   *declarative*   *interrogative*

3. How would you like to climb the summit?   *imperative*   *interrogative*

4. What a challenge that would be!   *declarative*   *exclamatory*

5. Find the height of the mountain and make a plan.   *declarative*   *imperative*

B. Read each sentence. If the punctuation is correct, write *correct* on the line. If it is incorrect, cross it out with an X. Then write the correct punctuation on the line.

1. Mark remembered the dangerous moment on the ice?   _____

2. Stay calm, Mark, no matter what.   _____

3. What would happen if he lost concentration for even one moment.   _____

4. Mark's father was content to stay at home.   _____

5. How much courage does it take to climb to the summit.   _____

6. Check all your equipment carefully.   _____

7. Will you be ready to start at dawn?   _____

8. The leader organized the rest of the team!   _____

9. Would he ever see a mountain as beautiful again.   _____

10. Alan ran four miles yesterday.   _____

THE FOUR TYPES OF SENTENCES

RETEACHING: A **declarative sentence** makes a statement. It ends with a period. An **interrogative sentence** asks a question. It ends with a question mark. An **imperative sentence** gives a command. It ends with a period or an exclamation point. An **exclamatory sentence** shows strong feeling. It ends with an exclamation point.

A. Write the correct punctuation mark at the end of each sentence. Then tell what kind of sentence it is.

1. On his trip, Mark has to do geometry problems

2. Where is his school

3. How distracted he is by the mountain summit in front of him

4. His mother insists that he work every day

5. Does anyone know how it feels to be facing the mountain

6. Pay attention and do some work, Mark

7. How tiring it is to concentrate

8. The thought of tomorrow's climb makes it difficult to work

9. You are going to be glad that you did your best

10. Will you get back to the base camp by tomorrow

B. Read the sentences below. Write the letter of the correct sentence type on the line. Then puncuate the sentences correctly.

1. _____ Panic is the cause of many accidents

2. _____ You must control your nerves

3. _____ What a rush I feel at the sight of the mountain

4. _____ What will happen if I fall

a. exclamatory

b. imperative

c. declarative

d. interrogative

THE FOUR TYPES OF SENTENCES

A. Decide the type of each sentence below. Fill in the circle next to the correct answer.

1. Never stop trying to succeed
   - (a) imperative
   - (b) interrogative
   - (c) declarative

2. How many mountains have you climbed
   - (a) declarative
   - (b) interrogative
   - (c) imperative

3. You may take a break now
   - (a) interrogative
   - (b) exclamatory
   - (c) imperative

4. What a beautiful sight that is
   - (a) exclamatory
   - (b) interrogative
   - (c) imperative

5. Follow the team leader
   - (a) exclamatory
   - (b) interrogative
   - (c) imperative

B. Is the punctuation in each sentence below correct? Fill in the circle next to the right answer.

1. How that mountain frightens me!
   - (a) .
   - (b) ?
   - (c) correct as is

2. The whole team is here to support you.
   - (a) ?
   - (b) !
   - (c) correct as is

3. Try harder, Mark.
   - (a) !
   - (b) ?
   - (c) correct as is

4. The team leaders and members met at the base camp!
   - (a) .
   - (b) ?
   - (c) correct as is

5. Will you start your climb at dawn!
   - (a) .
   - (b) ?
   - (c) correct as is

SIMPLE AND COMPOUND SENTENCES

> **RETEACHING:** A **simple sentence** is a sentence that expresses only one complete thought. A **compound sentence** is a sentence made up of two simple sentences joined by a comma and the word *and*, *but*, or *or*.

A. On the line, identify each sentence as either *simple* or *compound*.

1. Maizon will attend a new school soon. _____

2. Margaret and Maizon have been friends for a very long time. _____

3. Maizon is going to Blue Hill, but Margaret will stay behind. _____

4. She will leave soon, and she still has to pack. _____

5. This last summer with Maizon is a time of great change for the girls' friendship. _____

6. Maizon thinks of Margaret as her best friend in the whole world. _____

7. Sometimes things change, and they can't change back again. _____

8. The friendship may end, or it may stay the same. _____

B. Underline the simple sentences in each compound sentence below.

1. Ms. Tory held Margaret's hand, but she did not speak.

2. Maizon kept Margaret from doing things, but now Maizon is gone.

3. Margaret will try new things, or she will stay the same.

4. Margaret's dad died, and she lost her best friend.

5. The summer had brought sadness, and Margaret had suffered.

6. Next summer might be better, or it might be worse.

7. Margaret hoped for better times, but she couldn't count on them.

SIMPLE AND COMPOUND SENTENCES

Read each pair of sentences. Then make a compound sentence by joining the two sentences with a comma and a conjunction. Write the new sentence on the line provided.

1. Margaret's poem is long. It is not complicated.

   _____

2. Margaret does not discuss Maizon in this poem. She does tell about her father's death.

   _____

3. The poem mentions Margaret's mother. It quotes advice from Ms. Dell.

   _____

4. Margaret could have refused to write the poem. She could have refused to read it to the class.

   _____

5. The poem was well written. Ms. Peazle was proud of Margaret's efforts.

   _____

6. The class did not say anything about the poem. They did react to it.

   _____

7. Maybe no one knew what to say. Maybe the students were afraid to say the wrong thing.

   _____

8. The students were silent. Ms. Peazle knew what to write.

   _____

 On a separate piece of paper, write a paragraph about a time when a teacher or other adult helped you express your feelings or get over a sadness or disappointment. Include compound sentences in your paragraph.

8

SIMPLE AND COMPOUND SENTENCES

Are the underlined words punctuated correctly? Fill in the circle next to the right answer.

1. Ms. Dell is my favorite character and Ms. Peazle is Joan's.

   (a) character, and

   (b) character. And

   (c) correct as is

2. Ms. Dell is honest and gives good advice.

   (a) honest, and

   (b) honest. And

   (c) correct as is

3. She sometimes says painful, but important things to Margaret.

   (a) painful but

   (b) painful but,

   (c) correct as is

4. Maizon is sometimes a good friend but she can also be dishonest.

   (a) friend, but

   (b) friend but,

   (c) correct as is

5. She can charm Margaret or, she can hurt her.

   (a) Margaret, or

   (b) Margaret or

   (c) correct as is

6. Ms. Dell tells Margaret this gently but clearly.

   (a) gently, but clearly.

   (b) gently. But clearly.

   (c) correct as is

7. Margaret needs to learn the truth, or she will always have the wrong idea.

   (a) truth or

   (b) truth, or,

   (c) correct as is

8. Ms. Dell knows the truth and Hattie knows it too.

   (a) truth, and

   (b) truth. And

   (c) correct as is

9. Margaret will slowly but surely understand friends better.

   (a) slowly, but surely

   (b) slowly, but surely,

   (c) correct as is

10. Ms. Dell will help her grow up and understand the world.

    (a) up, and

    (b) up and,

    (c) correct as is

SENTENCE FRAGMENTS AND RUN-ONS

RETEACHING: A **sentence fragment** is a word group that has no subject or predicate or does not express a complete thought. A **run-on sentence** consists of two or more sentences joined without a conjunction.

A. Identify each of the following groups of words as a *fragment*, a *run-on,* or a *correct* sentence. **Draw a line to the right answer.**

1. When you first start to write a story you need to have an idea.

2. Where can you get ideas they come from so many places.

3. What you often need.

a. fragment

b. run-on

c. correct sentence

B. Rewrite the following fragments as correct sentences.

1. Helped him discover.

_____

2. Found in the library.

_____

3. Describes the things.

_____

4. His favorite tools.

_____

C. Rewrite the following run-ons as correct sentences.

1. His first attempts were poetry ideas came to him.

_____

2. One example is a poem about Mexico the poem was a short and funny one.

_____

3. He read and wrote poems, a few years later he started writing short stories.

_____

4. How did he create his characters he just invented them.

_____

SENTENCE FRAGMENTS AND RUN-ONS

RETEACHING: A **sentence fragment** is a word group that has no subject or predicate or does not express a complete thought. A **run-on sentence** consists of two or more sentences joined without a conjunction.

A. Read each group of words. Write *fragment* if the sentence is not complete. Write *run-on* if it consists of two or more sentences incorrectly joined. Write *correct* if it is a complete sentence.

1. To learn these things. _____

2. A typical working day. _____

3. Soto tries to get all the rest he needs. _____

4. Writing is like work it is hard work. _____

5. He spends many hours a day working his writing is his work. _____

B. Rewrite each fragment or run-on as a complete sentence.

1. Fresno, California, the home of Gary Soto and his family.

   _____

2. He grew up using his imagination this was how he became a writer.

   _____

3. It takes rest to have energy writing is difficult work.

   _____

4. Learning about language and words.

   _____

5. Life changed for Gary Soto when he went away to college suddenly everything was different.

   _____

   _____

SENTENCE FRAGMENTS AND RUN-ONS

Identify each group of words below. Fill in the circle next to the correct answer.

1. Writing is similar to other work.
   - (a) fragment
   - (b) run-on
   - (c) correct sentence

2. Writing demands energy it requires focus.
   - (a) fragment
   - (b) run-on
   - (c) correct sentence

3. Three or four hours a day writing.
   - (a) fragment
   - (b) run-on
   - (c) correct sentence

4. Start with a great idea, some ideas come from memories.
   - (a) fragment
   - (b) run-on
   - (c) correct sentence

5. Language and words and ideas.
   - (a) fragment
   - (b) run-on
   - (c) correct sentence

6. Make sure to set aside time for writing.
   - (a) fragment
   - (b) run-on
   - (c) correct sentence

7. Read the story aloud and see how it sounds add more if necessary.
   - (a) fragment
   - (b) run-on
   - (c) correct sentence

8. May need to add more.
   - (a) fragment
   - (b) run-on
   - (c) correct sentence

9. Sometimes special research is necessary sometimes imagination is enough.
   - (a) fragment
   - (b) run-on
   - (c) correct sentence

10. When growing up.
   - (a) fragment
   - (b) run-on
   - (c) correct sentence

SINGULAR AND PLURAL NOUNS

> **RETEACHING:** A noun can be **singular** or **plural**. Plural nouns often end in –s or –es. Some nouns may be the same in both the singular and plural forms. Other nouns form the plural in special ways.

A. Read the sentences below. Underline any singular nouns in each sentence once and any plural nouns twice.

1. The class read several articles about emergency medicine.

2. We read about workers who rescue very sick patients.

3. We learned that dispatchers make critical decisions when they answer a call.

4. A successful rescue requires the teamwork of different crews.

5. Some emergencies require both firefighters and paramedics.

B. Read the sentences below. Identify the underlined nouns in each sentence as either *singular* or *plural*.

1. Dispatchers must decide which crews to send to each emergency.

2. Operators must listen carefully because callers are often upset.

3. Life threatening accidents and illnesses occur at all hours of the day.

4. This means that transport vehicles and skilled technicians must be ready to go in the wink of an eye.

5. Fortunately, the well-trained employees of the emergency medical system started working at the scene more than thirty years ago!

Name

SINGULAR AND PLURAL NOUNS

RETEACHING: A **singular noun** names one person, place, thing, or idea. A **plural noun** names more than one person, place, thing, or idea. A plural noun is most often formed by adding –s to the singular. If a noun ends with s, ch, or x, a plural is formed by adding –es.

A. Write the plural form of each underlined singular noun on the line below each sentence.

1. A chopper might hold the key to saving the day!

   _____

2. The flight nurse moved the drug box closer to the infant.

   _____

3. The doctor treated a boy who was bitten by a spider.

   _____

4. The medic bent down to put a patch on his tray.

   _____

B. Fill in each empty box with the correct singular or plural noun.

SINGULAR NOUN	PLURAL NOUN
surgeon	
	helicopters
center	
	lungs
stretcher	
	backboards
baby	
turkey	
	families
class	

SINGULAR AND PLURAL NOUNS

Decide if the underlined nouns below are spelled correctly. Fill in the circle next to the right answer.

1. Four trucks transported the valuable medicine.

   (a) truck

   (b) truckes

   (c) correct as is

2. We take each accident seriously.

   (a) accidentes

   (b) accidents

   (c) correct as is

3. All of the worker were exhausted.

   (a) workers

   (b) workeries

   (c) correct as is

4. Ask the patient if she needs her glass to see.

   (a) glassess

   (b) glasses

   (c) correct as is

5. A helicopter arrived within minutes.

   (a) minute

   (b) minuties

   (c) correct as is

6. The paramedic assessed the victim's multiple injury.

   (a) injuryies

   (b) injuries

   (c) correct as is

7. Acute illness come on suddenly.

   (a) illnessies

   (b) illnesses

   (c) correct as is

8. Paramedics placed splint on the patient's legs.

   (a) splints

   (b) splintes

   (c) correct as is

9. Project Orbis helps patients in developing nation.

   (a) nationes

   (b) nations

   (c) correct as is

10. The Red Cross helps during emergency.

    (a) emergencies

    (b) emergences

    (c) correct as is

POSSESSIVE NOUNS

RETEACHING: A **possessive noun** shows ownership. To form the possessive of a singular noun, including those ending in s, x, and z, add 's. To form the possessive of a plural noun ending in s, add an apostrophe. To form the possessive of a plural noun that does not end in s, add 's.

A. **Read the sentences below. Underline singular possessives once and plural possessives twice.**

1. Brian Robeson's adventure took place in Canada's wilderness.

2. The pilot's heart attack prevented Brian from reaching his father's house.

3. Brian thought his parents' television set would broadcast news of his disappearance.

4. The plane's cables formed a "birdcage" that almost trapped him underwater.

5. After one hard day's work Brian's efforts paid off.

B. **Read the sentences below. Identify the underlined noun in each sentence as either** *singular possessive* **or** *plural possessive.*

1. The forest's beauty filled Brian with awe.   _____

2. The problems' solutions became apparent when Brian relaxed.   _____

3. Thoughts of the survival pack's contents kept Brian going.   _____

4. Brian cleaned away the fuselage's whole side and top.   _____

5. This boy's good sense kept him alive in the wilderness!   _____

Research and write five interesting facts about the wilderness. Use a possessive noun for each fact that you write.

POSSESSIVE NOUNS

A. Underline the correct form of the possessive noun in each sentence below.

1. (Charles's, Charles') story entertained his entire class.

2. The path led to the (Photography Association's, Photography Associations') cabin.

3. (Kendra Hawkers', Kendra Hawker's) vivid photos highlight animal habitats.

4. Sam set his (video club's, video clubs') equipment at the edge of the forest.

5. Several students participated in the (newspapers', newspaper's) photography contest.

6. The two (photographers', photographer's) portfolios were filled with interesting photos.

B. Read each sentence below. Then write the possessive noun and the word that it identifies on the line.

1. The painters' conference was in Boston. _____

2. Mrs. Raulerson's statements were concise. _____

3. The boxes' contents spilled out of their tops. _____

4. Venus's atmosphere does not contain oxygen. _____

5. The player's attitude helped her team. _____

6. Mr. Roqmoore's presence was highly valued. _____

POSSESSIVE NOUNS

Is the underlined possessive noun correct? Fill in the circle next to the right answer.

1. The survivors' good sense helped him solve problems.
   - (a) survivor's
   - (b) survivors's
   - (c) correct as is

2. The mosquitoes' attack escaped Brian's notice.
   - (a) mosquitoes
   - (b) mosquitos'
   - (c) correct as is

3. The young mans' adventure was filled with challenges.
   - (a) men
   - (b) man's
   - (c) correct as is

4. Mrs. Robesons parting gift helped her son survive.
   - (a) Robesons'
   - (b) Robeson's
   - (c) correct as is

5. *Hatchet* is Chris's favorite novel.
   - (a) Chris'
   - (b) Chris
   - (c) correct as is

6. The planes's tail did not sink.
   - (a) planes'
   - (b) plane's
   - (c) correct as is

7. The American Library Associations list of award winners is filled with adventure stories.
   - (a) American Library Associations'
   - (b) American Library Association's
   - (c) correct as is

8. The girl's group returned with armloads of adventure stories.
   - (a) girls's
   - (b) girls
   - (c) correct as is

9. Mrs. Jones's class just finished reading *Hatchet*.
   - (a) Mrs. Jone's
   - (b) Mrs. Jones
   - (c) correct as is

10. Many people have favorable opinions of Gary Paulsons' books.
    - (a) Paulson's
    - (b) Paulsons's
    - (c) correct as is

CAPITALIZING PROPER NOUNS AND ADJECTIVES

A. Read the following sentences. Circle the proper noun(s) and adjective(s) in each sentence. Then on the line write whether the circled word(s) is either a *proper noun* or a *proper adjective*.

1. William Butler Yeats wrote beautiful poetry! _____

2. He wrote the poem, The Lake Isle of Innisfree. _____

3. This Irish land must be quite special to the poem's author. _____

4. The place of which Yeats wrote is near Sligo, Ireland. _____

5. The sights beyond the lake include views of the Lough Gill Mountains. _____

6. The Hazelwood Sculpture Trail is close to the lake. _____

B. Fill in each empty box below with the corrct proper noun or proper adjective. The first one has been done for you.

PROPER NOUN	PROPER ADJECTIVE
Japan	Japanese
	American
Armenia	
	Taiwanese
Ireland	
	Polish
Hawaii	

CAPITALIZING PROPER NOUNS AND ADJECTIVES

Rewrite each sentence below correctly by capitalizing all the proper nouns and proper adjectives.

> A **proper noun** names a specific person, place, or thing. It begins with a capital letter. If a proper noun is more than one word, each important word is capitalized. A **proper adjective** is an adjective formed from a proper noun. Like a proper noun, it begins with a capital letter.

1. Last friday, ms. goldman's class went to the museum of science.

   _____

2. There is a beautiful building located at 525 shelton boulevard.

   _____

3. It was built sometime between world war II and the korean war.

   _____

4. Is it next to the thai restaurant called siam delight?

   _____

5. Is it across from the midwood professional building?

   _____

6. Do we have to take johnson parkway to get there, zach?

   _____

7. Will we pass by greenleaf associates where my aunt kim works?

   _____

8. At the museum, a chinese-american scientist spoke to us.

   _____

9. Her name is professor amy chow, and she is a friend of my uncle.

   _____

10. She grew up in hong kong and later moved to the united states of america.

   _____

Read a book about survival skills. On a separate sheet of paper, write three sentences about the book. Be sure to capitalize proper nouns and adjectives.

CAPITALIZING PROPER NOUNS AND ADJECTIVES

Decide if the underlined proper nouns and adjectives are capitalized correctly. Fill in the circle next to the right answer.

1. The hazelwood sculpture trail is near the lake.

   (a) Hazelwood Sculpture Trail

   (b) Hazelwood sculpture trail

   (c) correct as is

2. The peaks of the Ox Mountains are visible from the lake.

   (a) ox mountains

   (b) Ox mountains

   (c) correct as is

3. William butler Yeats was the author of many poems.

   (a) William Butler yeats

   (b) William Butler Yeats

   (c) correct as is

4. Ask the tourist if she has ever met an australian before.

   (a) Australia

   (b) Australian

   (c) correct as is

5. Within moments the African diplomat arrived.

   (a) african

   (b) Africa

   (c) correct as is

6. Dr. Sanchez makes periodic trips to the aleutian islands.

   (a) Aleutian islands

   (b) Aleutian Islands

   (c) correct as is

7. The Peruvian topography becomes rugged when you enter the mountains.

   (a) Peru

   (b) peruvian

   (c) correct as is

8. Sylvester is a californian.

   (a) Californian

   (b) California

   (c) correct as is

9. Floridians enjoy many water sports.

   (a) florida

   (b) Florida

   (c) correct as is

10. Ricardo is learning to speak japanese.

    (a) Japanese

    (b) Japan

    (c) correct as is

CAPITALIZING AND PUNCTUATING ABBREVIATIONS

RETEACHING: An **abbreviation** is a shortened form of a word or phrase. The abbreviations of proper nouns most often begin with a capital letter and end with a period. Some lowercase nouns, such as compass directions, are abbreviated using capital letters, without space between, and no periods.

A. Underline the abbreviations in each sentence. Then write down the word or words for which each abbreviation stands.

1. Rockaway Rd. and Lower Woods Tr. are on the map in the Wayfinding Book.

   _____

2. A compass showing NE, SW, and other directions appears near the map.

   _____

3. The Caroline Islanders used starmaps to find N, S, E, and W while navigating through the Pacific Islands. _____

4. The Wayfinding Book includes a streetmap of Atlanta, GA. _____

5. This book was written by Mrs. Vicki McVey. _____

6. The author suggests that it is important to use pathfinders whether you are walking on Park Ave. or hiking on Grandfather Mtn. _____

B. Fill in each of the blanks below with the correct abbreviation of the word given in parentheses.

1. _____ and _____ Smith enjoy wilderness hiking. (Mister, Missus)

2. _____ 488 leads into Great Basin National Park wilderness lands. (Route)

3. Quadna _____ near Grand Rapids, offers wilderness skiing. (Mountain)

4. _____ Vetna visits Quadna Mountain every year. (Doctor)

5. He meets his friends at 1611 Woolburne _____ and proceeds to the mountain. (Street)

6. His skiing partners include Craig Brown, _____, and Craig Brown, _____. (Junior, Senior)

7. They will travel along Ridgemoore _____ and then head _____ (Boulevard, northeast) until they reach the mountain.

CAPITALIZING AND PUNCTUATING ABBREVIATIONS

A. Fill in the chart with the correct abbreviations or acronyms. Use correct capitalization and punctuation.

RETEACHING: An **abbreviation** is a shortened form of a word or phrase. The abbreviations of proper nouns most often begin with a capital letter and end with a period. Some lowercase nouns, such as compass directions, are abbreviated using capital letters, without space between, and no periods.

	Abbreviation		Abbreviation
1. doctor d chang		11. mrs m dyson	
2. mr b white jr		12. dr c katz sr	
3. 10 thoreau rd		13. route 109	
4. hanscom blvd		14. elm street	
5. oak avenue		15. mount royal	
6. troy new york		16. dayton ohio	
7. moab utah		17. boise idaho	
8. Friday, January 4, 7 in the morning		18. Monday, August 9, 6 at night	
9. connecticut street southeast		19. massachusetts avenue northwest	
10. p.i.n.		20. t.v.	

B. Rewrite this address correctly for an envelope. Use abbreviations.

    doctor owen russell senior
    huntington lakes apartments
    4432 Sunshine boulevard
    del ray beach florida 33446

On a separate sheet of paper, list the names, addresses, and birthdates of five friends and relatives. Use abbreviations.

CAPITALIZING AND
PUNCTUATING ABBREVIATIONS

Decide if there is an error in the underlined words below. Fill in the circle next to the correct answer.

1. mrs r charles enjoys wilderness trekking.
   - (a) Mrs. R. Charles
   - (b) mrs. R. charles
   - (c) correct as is

2. We take redwing rd to Mt. Hinson.
   - (a) Redwing rd
   - (b) Redwing Rd.
   - (c) correct as is

3. Charlotte walked the length of maple blvd.
   - (a) maple Blvd
   - (b) Maple Blvd.
   - (c) correct as is

4. mr. T white showed us the route.
   - (a) Mr. T White
   - (b) Mr. T. White
   - (c) correct as is

5. A hiker reached the lodge at ox mountain.
   - (a) Ox Mountain
   - (b) Ox mountain
   - (c) correct as is

6. Dr. Southern lives on green st.
   - (a) Green st.
   - (b) Green St.
   - (c) correct as is

7. dr albert evans sr. lives at Westfield Circle.
   - (a) Dr. albert Evans Sr.
   - (b) Dr. Albert Evans, Sr.,
   - (c) correct as is

8. Penelope St. is se of Westmoor Place.
   - (a) SE
   - (b) S.E.
   - (c) correct as is

9. The hike was set for tues., jan. 3rd.
   - (a) Tues., Jan 3rd
   - (b) Tues., Jan. 3rd
   - (c) correct as is

10. The hiking club meets at lakefront apartments.
   - (a) Lakefront Apartments
   - (b) Lakefront apartments
   - (c) correct as is

ACTION VERBS WITH DIRECT OBJECTS

RETEACHING: An **action verb** is a word that shows action. It can be the simple predicate of the sentence. A **direct object** is a noun or pronoun that follows an action verb. It receives the action.

A. Read the sentences below. Underline the action verb in each sentence.

1. At the drugstore, Rufus picks up the small tube of toothpaste.

2. He looks carefully at the price tag on the tube.

3. Next, he grabs another tube off the shelf.

4. He sees the price on that one too.

5. He knows the cost of the ingredients in paste.

6. He makes his own paste at home.

B. Complete the following sentences with an action verb.

1. Kate _____ the eye shadow on the shelf.

2. She _____ that the price was high for such a small thing.

3. She _____ not to buy it that day.

4. Her friends _____ eye shadow all the time.

On a separate piece of paper, write a paragraph describing the last time you went shopping. Try to include as many action verbs as possible.

ACTION VERBS WITH DIRECT OBJECTS

RETEACHING: An **action verb** is a word that shows action. It can be the simple predicate of the sentence. A **direct object** is a noun or pronoun that follows an action verb. It receives the action.

A. Read the sentences below. Underline the direct object that follows an action verb in each sentence.

1. Rufus finished his experiments with paste and flavors.

2. Kate tasted the samples in the kitchen.

3. He handed an almond-flavored paste to Kate.

4. Rufus proposed a better idea.

5. Carefully, he packed the pan with his new toothpaste.

6. He asked a question about the population of the United States.

B. Complete each of the following sentences with a direct object.

1. Rufus and Kate rode _____

2. They made _____

3. The class gave _____

4. Kate's father knew _____

 On a separate sheet of paper, write a paragraph about a product you use because it is inexpensive and works well. Underline the action verbs and circle the direct objects.

ACTION VERBS WITH DIRECT OBJECTS

Identify the underlined word or words in each sentence.
Fill in the circle next to the correct answer.

1. Rufus finished breakfast early that morning.

   (a) action verb
   (b) direct object
   (c) neither

2. He asked the question in math class.

   (a) action verb
   (b) direct object
   (c) neither

3. Her father knows the answers to many questions.

   (a) action verb
   (b) direct object
   (c) neither

4. She enjoyed math class that day.

   (a) action verb
   (b) direct object
   (c) neither

5. The drug store sells many tubes of toothpaste.

   (a) action verb
   (b) direct object
   (c) neither

6. The class worked out the problem.

   (a) action verb
   (b) direct object
   (c) neither

7. Everyone watched the program.

   (a) action verb
   (b) direct object
   (c) neither

8. Most customers like the product.

   (a) action verb
   (b) direct object
   (c) neither

9. Joe interviews people with hobbies.

   (a) action verb
   (b) direct object
   (c) neither

10. Rufus packed the toothpaste in jars.

    (a) action verb
    (b) direct object
    (c) neither

LINKING VERBS

A. Read each sentence below. Circle the linking verb and underline the predicate noun or predicate adjective in each.

1. Most of the new flavors tasted delicious.

2. Bubble gum was an unusual flavor.

3. The ice cream was always fresh.

4. Ice cream is a special treat for many people.

5. Some flavors became famous.

6. Others, like a garlic flavored one, were unsuccessful.

B. Read the sentences below carefully. Identify the underlined words as *linking verbs, predicate nouns,* or a *predicate adjectives*.

1. Ben and Jerry were the founders of a new company. _____

2. The whole place smelled fresh. _____

3. The company grew larger every year. _____

4. Sometimes, their responsibilities seemed endless. _____

5. However, the new business was satisfying. _____

6. The store became a regular stop for many visitors. _____

7. They were proud of their achievement. _____

LINKING VERBS

A. Read the following sentences. Underline each linking verb. If a sentence contains a predicate noun or predicate adjective, circle it.

1. Peppermint is a common herb.

2. Peppermint tea tastes great.

3. My peppermint shampoo smells good on my hair.

4. For years, peppermint has been my favorite plant.

5. Even its name sounds interesting!

B. Read the following sentences. Circle each linking verb. If a sentence contains a predicate noun, underline it once. If it contains a predicate adjective, underline it twice.

1. Ben & Jerry's is a huge company in Vermont.

2. Vermont is a beautiful state.

3. In the fall, it looks especially dazzling.

4. Nevertheless, the winters seem harsh.

5. Vermont maple syrup tastes sweet.

6. Its dairy products seem so fresh!

7. In the summer, the hillsides appear a rich, dark green.

8. For new beginnings, Vermont has been a favorite place.

9. It has been a popular skiing destination.

10. To me, Vermont sounds very attractive.

 On a separate piece of paper, write two sentences about your favorite flavor of ice cream. Use linking verbs in your sentences.

LINKING VERBS

Identify the underlined word in each sentence below.
Fill in the circle next to the correct answer.

1. Running a business was a team **effort**.
   - (a) linking verb
   - (b) predicate noun
   - (c) predicate adjective

2. Ben and Jerry **are** serious about helping others.
   - (a) linking verb
   - (b) predicate noun
   - (c) predicate adjective

3. They are **proud** of their achievement.
   - (a) linking verb
   - (b) predicate noun
   - (c) predicate adjective

4. Each employee is a **member** of the team.
   - (a) linking verb
   - (b) predicate noun
   - (c) predicate adjective

5. The customers seem **happy**.
   - (a) linking verb
   - (b) predicate noun
   - (c) predicate adjective

6. Their store is a favorite **place** for tourists.
   - (a) linking verb
   - (b) predicate noun
   - (c) predicate adjective

7. Communication **is** an important part of teamwork.
   - (a) linking verb
   - (b) predicate noun
   - (c) predicate adjective

8. Incentives are one **way** to encourage people.
   - (a) linking verb
   - (b) predicate noun
   - (c) predicate adjective

9. From the start, they **seemed** to succeed.
   - (a) linking verb
   - (b) predicate noun
   - (c) predicate adjective

10. To Ben and Jerry, it **was** the perfect spot.
    - (a) linking verb
    - (b) predicate noun
    - (c) predicate adjective

PRESENT, PAST, AND FUTURE TENSES

Read each sentence carefully. Identify the underlined verb as *past*, *present*, or *future* tense.

> **RETEACHING:** The **tense** of a verb shows the time of the action. The **present tense** shows that the action is happening now. The **past tense** shows that the action happened in the past. The **future tense** shows the action will happen in the future. It uses the helping verb *will* followed by a main verb.

1. Merchandisers start by listening to focus groups. _____

2. They bring together many styles for teenagers to look at. _____

3. Later, the design team will add special touches. _____

4. They sent the first designs out for more work. _____

5. The marketers discuss the latest fashions and ideas. _____

6. They keep the prices down so teenagers can afford them. _____

7. At one point, the patterns were sent back to the cutting room. _____

8. There, sewers assemble a small run for the test market. _____

9. A new pair of jeans will appear in no time. _____

10. Shoppers of all ages will buy the jeans. _____

11. The marketers decide on a plan for letting customers know about the jeans. _____

12. Then, they will plan a campaign to attract buyers. _____

13. For instance, they designed the big signs and size charts you see in stores. _____

14. An ad agency will create ads for magazines and newspapers. _____

15. Researchers will show their ads to consumer groups. _____

PRESENT, PAST, AND FUTURE TENSES

On the line provided, write the correct tense of the verb given in parentheses.

1. We _____ at many styles of jeans. (look; past)

2. We _____ for hours! (shop; past)

3. Jeans _____ in so many styles. (come; present)

4. Paula _____ the wide-cut look. (like; present)

5. I _____ on jeans with a straighter, tighter leg. (try; past)

6. Paula _____ her jeans super long. (wear; future)

7. Long ago, she _____ her jeans, but not anymore. (hem; past)

8. Styles _____ quickly. (change; present)

9. The jeans business constantly _____ new styles. (supply; present)

10. This year's look _____ next year's laugh. (be; future)

11. Most stores _____ jeans in a variety of sizes. (carry; present)

12. Tomorrow Paula and her friends _____ to the mall to shop. (go; future)

On a separate piece of paper, write a paragraph about a product or style you bought or used in the past that you no longer enjoy. Underline each verb you use.

PRESENT, PAST, AND FUTURE TENSES

Identify the underlined word or words in each sentence.
Fill in the circle next to the correct answer.

1. Merchandisers find styles as well as fabric.

   (a) present

   (b) past

   (c) future

2. Teenagers will go to malls to buy them.

   (a) present

   (b) past

   (c) future

3. First the merchandisers traveled to the big stores.

   (a) present

   (b) past

   (c) future

4. Then, teenagers will decide what to buy.

   (a) present

   (b) past

   (c) future

5. The team will design the best fitting jeans.

   (a) present

   (b) past

   (c) future

6. Later the teams will meet with the designers about a plan.

   (a) present

   (b) past

   (c) future

7. On busy days clerks fold many pairs of jeans.

   (a) present

   (b) past

   (c) future

8. They keep the jeans neat and clean.

   (a) present

   (b) past

   (c) future

9. Thousands of jeans were sold last year.

   (a) present

   (b) past

   (c) future

10. Designers gather all the information.

    (a) present

    (b) past

    (c) future

IRREGULAR VERBS AND PAST PARTICIPLES

A. On the line, write the past tense form of the irregular verb in parentheses.

1. Sarah Ida (grow) tired of looking for a job. _____

2. She (see) the shoeshine man's sign. _____

3. The shoeshine man (give) Sarah Ida a job. _____

4. He (say) yes to her question about work. _____

5. He (tell) her to come back the next day. _____

6. That's how Sarah Ida (become) a shoeshine girl. _____

7. Sometimes Sarah Ida (do) a good job. _____

8. She (lose) the shoeshine man at least one customer. _____

B. On the line, write the past participle form of the irregular verb in parentheses.

1. Sarah Ida had (grow) tired of looking for a job. _____

2. Someone has (see) the shoeshine man's sign. _____

3. Who has (give) Sarah Ida a job? _____

4. Had he (say) yes to Sarah Ida? _____

5. He had (tell) her about his work. _____

6. Sarah had (become) frustrated looking for a job. _____

7. By the end of the story, she will have (lose) some of her nastiness. _____

8. She had not (think) much about this kind of job before. _____

9. Sarah had (make) a new friend of the shoeshine man. _____

10. She has (write) to a friend about her new job. _____

IRREGULAR VERBS AND PAST PARTICIPLES

A. Complete the chart below by adding the past tense and past participle form of each verb.

Verb	Past Tense	Past Participle (with *have* or *had*)
1. become		
2. buy		
3. break		
4. choose		
5. do		
6. give		
7. make		
8. see		
9. sing		
10. speak		
11. swim		
12. write		

B. Write three sentences using the past tense or past participle form of the verbs listed in the chart above.

1. _____

2. _____

3. _____

On a separate sheet of paper, write a paragraph about things your friends have done in their spare time. Use at least five irregular past tense or past participle verb forms from the chart above.

PAST, PRESENT, AND FUTURE PERFECT TENSES

A. Underline the present perfect, past perfect, or future perfect verb in each sentence. Be sure to include the helping verb.

1. Sheila had done something new.

2. She had purchased snowshoes.

3. She has been reading about how to use them.

4. By next weekend, she will have gained some confidence.

5. By the end of the year, she will have tried them out in snow.

6. Going snowshoeing has been a goal of hers for years.

7. She had thought about buying snowshoes long before she ever got them.

B. On the line, tell whether the underlined verb is in the *present perfect*, *past perfect*, or *future perfect* tense.

1. Dave had looked at that brand many times before he bought it. _____

2. He has worn that brand of sneakers for years. _____

3. By the time he graduates next fall, he will have bought about forty pairs of those sneakers. _____

4. Sneakers have been the most popular footwear for decades. _____

5. I will have bought a new pair by next January. _____

6. We have been buying special cross-training sneakers for years. _____

7. My mother had worn tennis sneakers before she bought her first cross-trainers. _____

8. She has been so pleased with her new sneakers. _____

9. He had walked every day for a year before buying new sneakers. _____

10. By the end of the day, she will have run ten miles. _____

PAST, PRESENT, AND FUTURE PERFECT TENSES

A. On the line, write the present perfect form of the verb in parentheses.

1. Sam (earn) some money at his new job. _____

2. He (make) more than fifty dollars. _____

3. He (help) with work in their yards. _____

4. People (give) him lots of different chores. _____

B. On the line, write the past perfect form of the verb in parentheses.

1. Before he turned twelve, neighbors (ask)
   Sam for help with their lawns. _____

2. Before then, Sam (think) of doing yard work. _____

3. He (speak) with his mother about earning money. _____

4. She (say) yes to him before he got his first customer. _____

C. On the line, write the future perfect form of the verb in parentheses.

1. By June, Sam (earn) enough money for a new bike. _____

2. Perhaps, by then, he also (find) a new way to make money. _____

3. Malik (learn) many things by then. _____

4. Jenna (meet) all his friends. _____

5. With the help of his father, he (mow) all of his neighbors'
   lawns by the end of the week. _____

On a separate piece of paper, write a paragraph describing two goals that you will have achieved by the end of this summer.

SUBJECT AND OBJECT PRONOUNS

A. Read the sentences below. Identify the underlined pronoun as a *subject pronoun* or an *object pronoun*.

1. They lived long before the invention of writing. _____

2. We still know something about them. _____

3. For many years scientists have studied this. _____

4. She found what might be the footprints of a small child. _____

5. The print clearly belonged to him. _____

6. It is considered a fossil. _____

7. They are mostly skulls, bones, and teeth. _____

B. Read the sentences below. Fill in each blank with a pronoun that fits the sentence.

1. Cro-Magnons lived in modern Europe. Today, _____ are called modern humans.

2. Scientists study the lives of these people. They want to learn more about _____.

3. A fossil can be different things. It is created when rocks form around _____.

4. A fossil is like a clue. _____ tells scientists a story.

5. Cave artists did not sign their work. _____ lived long before writing was invented.

6. We are always trying to learn more about the paintings. They continue to fascinate _____.

7. The path led up to the cliff. _____ ended at a narrow ledge.

8. The three friends met one afternoon. _____ shared a love of adventure.

SUBJECT AND OBJECT PRONOUNS

Rewrite each sentence below. Replace the underlined words with the pronoun that fits the sentence.

> **RETEACHING:** A **subject pronoun** indicates who or what performs the action of a sentence. *I, you, he, she, it, they,* and *we* are subject pronouns. *This, that, these,* and *those* can also sometimes serve as subject pronouns. An **object pronoun** indicates who or what receives the action. *Me, you, him, her, it, us,* and *them* are object pronouns. *This, that, these,* and *those* can also sometimes serve as object pronouns.

SUBJECT PRONOUNS	OBJECT PRONOUNS
I, you, he, she, it, we, they *this, that, these, those*	*me, you, him, her, it, us, them* *this, that, these, those*

Select the correct pronoun from the chart above.

1. The early moderns made their own tools and weapons.

   _____

2. A fine pointed tool was used for engraving.

   _____

3. People needed food so they followed the animals.

   _____

4. Animals bones were used to make musical instruments.

   _____

5. Later, men and women would become painters and carvers.

   _____

6. For years, things remained equal between modern people and Neanderthals.

   _____

7. Neanderthals were no match for modern humans.

   _____

 On a separate piece of paper, write a paragraph describing the feelings archaeologists might have as they crawl along the floor of an ancient cave. What thoughts do you think they might have as they discover prehistoric paintings? Include as many subject and object pronouns as possible.

SUBJECT AND OBJECT PRONOUNS

Fill in the circle next to the pronoun that correctly replaces the underlined words.

1. Modern men became better hunters.
   - (a) They
   - (b) Them
   - (c) He

2. The man spent time looking for food.
   - (a) He
   - (b) We
   - (c) Those

3. The tree formed a shelter.
   - (a) It
   - (b) They
   - (c) Those

4. It was easy to spot the animals.
   - (a) it
   - (b) them
   - (c) those

5. Oak trees grow poorly here.
   - (a) Those
   - (b) They
   - (c) Them

6. Later, people invented the knife.
   - (a) these
   - (b) it
   - (c) them

7. You and I built it together.
   - (a) We
   - (b) Them
   - (c) They

8. We lit a fire to warm the woman.
   - (a) us
   - (b) her
   - (c) she

9. They found a new use for fire.
   - (a) them
   - (b) it
   - (c) those

10. It made a big difference to the people.
    - (a) them
    - (b) those
    - (c) they

POSSESSIVE PRONOUNS

A. Complete each sentence below with a possessive pronoun that fits the sentence.

RETEACHING: A **possessive pronoun** is a pronoun that shows ownership. The possessive pronouns *my, your, her, our, its,* and *their* come before nouns. The pronouns *mine, yours, hers, ours,* and *theirs* stand alone. *His* can be used both ways.

1. He woke to hear the laughter of _____ friends.

2. He could hear sellers describing _____ wares.

3. The athletes marched into _____ stadium.

4. "We heard the names of _____ teammates being called."

5. "I think I heard _____ brother's name."

6. The other Athenians heard _____ names.

7. We felt _____ own hearts swell with pride.

8. "Charioteers and horse riders, today will be _____ day."

9. He thought to himself, "I am next. Now it is _____ turn."

10. He could tell that _____ friend was nervous.

B. Read the first sentence. Then choose a possessive pronoun that makes sense in the second sentence.

yours   hers   his   mine   theirs

1. You know your own name. It is _____.

2. I brought my trumpet. It is _____.

3. She has her winner's wreath. It is _____.

4. He had his own ideas. They were _____.

5. They were proud of the work. It was _____.

6. I own the bike. It is _____.

7. José built the model. It is _____.

8. You found the shells. They are _____.

POSSESSIVE PRONOUNS

A. Read the sentences below carefully. Underline the possessive pronouns. If a sentence has no possessive pronoun, write *none* after the sentence.

1. She knew that her turn to run would come soon.

2. The first race is always the hardest for our team.

3. Mine was the third race.

4. She knew her parents would be proud.

5. It was their idea that she enter the contest.

6. Her mother said that it made her life happier.

7. Their trainer worked all the racers very hard.

8. My friend said that his trainer was strict too.

9. The trophy held its power over them.

10. If it were mine, I would be proud to own it.

11. I hoped that he would win.

12. Long ago, she learned to set her pace early in the race.

13. I am sorry that his son lost the race.

14. Ours was the best all around team.

15. Mine was the proudest moment.

B. Rewrite these sentences using possessive pronouns.

1. Mrs. Clark went to John's first race.

_____

2. She saw that the team's trainer was standing ready.

_____

3. She was worried that John's injury was painful.

_____

POSSESSIVE PRONOUNS

Decide if the underlined possessive pronoun is correct. Fill in the circle next to the right answer.

1. He felt someone touch his hand.

   (a) her

   (b) their

   (c) correct as is

2. The runners came out through theirs own entrance.

   (a) their

   (b) mine

   (c) correct as is

3. He heard the cheers of its own friends.

   (a) his

   (b) her

   (c) correct as is

4. She raised her arm to begin the race.

   (a) his

   (b) their

   (c) correct as is

5. The boys took their places at the starting line.

   (a) his

   (b) her

   (c) correct as is

6. He said to himself, "This is mine only chance."

   (a) its

   (b) my

   (c) correct as is

7. We knew it would soon be our turn to run.

   (a) my

   (b) mine

   (c) correct as is

8. Our was the team that was favored to win.

   (a) Their

   (b) Ours

   (c) correct as is

9. He felt the blood rush to her ears.

   (a) his

   (b) their

   (c) correct as is

10. The onlookers raised their voices.

    (a) theirs

    (b) his

    (c) correct as is

INDEFINITE PRONOUNS

A. Underline the indefinite pronoun in each sentence.

1. Many enjoy landscape paintings.

2. Landscape paintings show some.

3. All show outdoor scenes.

4. Several of those paintings depict ocean scenes.

5. Everyone likes to look at watercolors.

6. Does anyone know the name of this painting?

7. The guide explained the painting to everybody.

8. Somebody said it was by Winslow Homer.

9. Few of us knew anything about his paintings.

10. In fact, I had never seen any.

B. On the line, write whether the underlined pronoun is *indefinite* or *not indefinite*.

1. Someone painted a picture of a tiger. _____

2. It was a kindly looking animal. _____

3. Mark showed the painting to someone in his class. _____

4. He said it was an excellent likeness of a tiger. _____

5. No one believed the tiger could ever become real. _____

6. Some of us laughed at the thought of that. _____

7. Everyone knows that paintings can't come to life. _____

8. Even though some paintings look real, none are. _____

9. The girl believed that her painting was the most realistic. _____

10. Most of them should not be believed. _____

INDEFINITE PRONOUNS

A. On the line, write the antecedent of each underlined pronoun.

1. Mary Cassatt was a painter.
   She was an American. _____

2. Cassatt painted boating scenes. They show well-dressed
   men and women. _____

3. I like the painting of two people in a boat. It has
   beautiful blues. _____

4. Cassatt is a famous painter. People go to museums to see her work. _____

5. Edward Degas was a painter, too. He often painted ballerinas. _____

6. The paintings are full of light. They have surprising
   green and yellow colors. _____

7. The paintings are in museums. You can see them. _____

B. In each sentence below, circle the pronoun that agrees with the underlined antecedent.

1. Everyone brought (his or her, their) paintbrushes.

2. Many children brought (his or her, their) paints.

3. Someone painted (his or her, their) first picture.

4. Everybody had (his or her, their) eyes on the lake.

5. No one liked (his or her, their) finished art work!

6. Several girls crumpled up (her, their) drawings.

7. Each of the students had (his or her, their) own problems trying to paint!

On a separate piece of paper, write about a painting, photo, or other picture that everyone—or no one—in your family likes. Be sure the pronouns you use agree with their antecedents.

INDEFINITE PRONOUNS

Are the underlined pronouns correct? Fill in the circle next to the right answer.

1. Ben took the test. It was difficult.
   - (a) He was
   - (b) They were
   - (c) correct as is

2. Everyone had their pencils ready.
   - (a) his or her
   - (b) her
   - (c) correct as is

3. No one brought his or her dictionary.
   - (a) his
   - (b) their
   - (c) correct as is

4. Ella finished the test quickly. They were easy!
   - (a) It was
   - (b) She was
   - (c) correct as is

5. Mark worked on the test slowly. She was confused.
   - (a) He
   - (b) It
   - (c) correct as is

6. Everybody did their best.
   - (a) his or her
   - (b) her
   - (c) correct as is

7. Another student gave Kyle a pencil when his broke.
   - (a) any
   - (b) her
   - (c) correct as is

8. A boy was kind to Andy, so he thanked them.
   - (a) him
   - (b) him or her
   - (c) correct as is

9. Rosa was encouraging. She patted me on the back.
   - (a) He
   - (b) They
   - (c) correct as is

10. Each of the students in my class received their scores yesterday.
   - (a) his
   - (b) his or her
   - (c) correct as is

SUBJECT-VERB AGREEMENT

RETEACHING: A **subject** and **verb** in a sentence must agree in person (first, second, or third) and in number. Many singular subjects agree with regular present tense verbs that end in –s or –es. Plural subjects, compound subjects, and the singular subjects *I* and *you* agree with present tense verbs that do not add these endings.

A. In the chart below, write the correct form of the regular present tense verb.

Verb	Agrees With Plural Subjects Compound Subjects, *I* and *You*	Agrees With *He, She, It,* and Other Singular Subjects
1. show		
2. learn		
3. touch		
4. feel		
5. discuss		
6. prefer		
7. need		
8. miss		
9. like		
10. write		

B. Write the form of the verb in parentheses that agrees with each subject.

1. Sean (leave) _____
2. Bob and Katrina (whisper) _____
3. football (sail) _____
4. he (think) _____
5. they (sing) _____

6. it (bounce) _____
7. Mr. and Mrs. Chen (listen) _____
8. cars (pass) _____
9. Olivia (watch) _____
10. teacher (dismiss) _____

SUBJECT-VERB AGREEMENT

> **RETEACHING:** A **subject** and **verb** in a sentence must agree in person (first, second, or third) and in number. Many singular subjects agree with regular present tense verbs that end in –s or –es. Plural subjects, compound subjects, and the singular subjects *I* and *you* agree with present tense verbs that do not add these endings.

A. In the chart, write the correct form of *be*.

Agrees With *I*	Agrees With *You*	Agrees With Plural and Compound Subjects	Agrees With *He, She, It,* and Other Singular Subjects

B. In the chart, write the correct form of the irregular present tense verb.

Verb	Agrees With Plural Subjects, Compound Subjects, *I* and *You*	Agrees With *He, She, It,* and Other Singular Subjects
1. do		
2. have		
3. go		

C. On the line, write the form of the irregular verb in parentheses that agrees with the subject.

1. Lauren (have) the book. _____

2. Zach and Tom (do) the work. _____

3. We (be) on the bus. _____

4. The ball (go) a long way. _____

5. I (be) the captain. _____

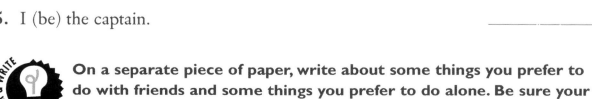

On a separate piece of paper, write about some things you prefer to do with friends and some things you prefer to do alone. Be sure your subjects and verbs agree.

SUBJECT-VERB AGREEMENT

Are the underlined verbs correct? Fill in the circle next to the right answer.

1. The book is open.
   - (a) are
   - (b) am
   - (c) correct as is

2. Tammy and Don looks at it.
   - (a) look
   - (b) lookes
   - (c) correct as is

3. They study the pictures from Ancient Egypt.
   - (a) studies
   - (b) studying
   - (c) correct as is

4. Mummies and pyramids interests them.
   - (a) interest
   - (b) interestes
   - (c) correct as is

5. The book discusses ancient building methods.
   - (a) discuss
   - (b) discuss's
   - (c) correct as is

6. It explaines how the pyramids were built.
   - (a) explains
   - (b) explain
   - (c) correct as is

7. Don wish for a trip back in time.
   - (a) wishs
   - (b) wishes
   - (c) correct as is

8. Sometimes the past seems more interesting than the present.
   - (a) seem
   - (b) seemes
   - (c) correct as is

9. People has easier lives in modern times than in the past.
   - (a) had
   - (b) have
   - (c) correct as is

10. They lives longer, healthier lives.
    - (a) liveses
    - (b) live
    - (c) correct as is

ADJECTIVES

Read the following sentences. Underline each adjective, including articles. If a sentence contains a demonstrative adjective, circle it.

> **RETEACHING:** An **adjective** is a word that describes a noun or pronoun. The adjectives *a, an*, and *the* are articles. The words *this, that, these,* and *those* are **demonstrative adjectives** when they come before a noun that they point out or refer to.

1. Did you see that show at the National Postal Museum?

2. It is about the mail compartment on the *Titanic*.

3. It shows an old room with sea creatures growing in it.

4. That huge room contained thousands of letters.

5. The post office believes some of these letters could actually still be deliverable!

6. This interesting exhibit explains many problems related to the old mail.

7. First of all, these letters have been on the sea floor for about one hundred years.

8. Still, the post office must deliver all posted mail.

9. How will it find the relatives of those people?

10. What an expensive, difficult task it will be!

11. Still, could information in one of those letters change someone's life?

12. Could it solve a mystery or cure a broken heart?

13. Are valuable items in those decaying letters and packages?

14. Dealing with this mail will not be an easy task.

15. Yet, it does promise to be an exciting and fascinating one.

 On a separate piece of paper, write a paragraph describing a luxury plane, ship, or train that you would like to ride on. Write a paragraph describing it. Invent details if you need to, and use vivid adjectives.

ADVERBS

Read the following sentences. Underline each adverb. Then write whether the adverb tells *how*, *when*, or *where*.

1. Here is a newsstand. _____

2. I haven't read the paper today. _____

3. First, let's read the headlines. _____

4. This one sounds extremely urgent. _____

5. The writer clearly explains the effects of a tidal wave. _____

6. It hit yesterday in Japan. _____

7. Tragically, many homes were suddenly and totally destroyed. _____

8. People in the area need help badly. _____

9. It says here that help is on its way now. _____

10. I sincerely hope it gets there soon! _____

11. The deer quickly darted into the forest. _____

12. I'm meeting friends early. _____

13. Angela fell down after catching the ball. _____

On a separate piece of paper, write about either a recent local news event or about a national news story. Use adverbs that tell *how*, *where*, and *when*.

PREPOSITIONS AND PREPOSITIONAL PHRASES

A. Each of the following sentences contains at least one prepositional phrase. Underline each phrase. Then, on the line, write *adjective* if it is an adjective phrase or *adverb* if it is an adverb phrase.

1. We listen to the radio. _____

2. A radio by my side makes work easier. _____

3. I play the radio at all hours. _____

4. Some people prefer a radio with headphones. _____

5. Someday, I would like a job in radio. _____

B. Look at the underlined object in each sentence below. If it is correct, write *correct*. If not, write the appropriate object on the line.

1. Michelle recommended the radio show to Abe and I. _____

2. Abe and I listened to it with Pete and she. _____

3. For Abe and me, it was a lot of fun. _____

4. In fact, it was fun for them and us. _____

5. Between you and I, there are three radios. _____

6. They sent the newspaper to Josh and I. _____

BUILDING SENTENCES

A. Underline each independent clause once and each dependent clause twice.

1. The white rabbit is an important character in this story.

2. The hatter is called a hatter because he makes hats.

3. When people use the word *knave* to talk about cards, they refer to a jack.

4. The word *knave* has other meanings, but it usually refers to "a sly person."

5. The knave is on trial although it seems clear that he did not commit a crime.

6. Although he has a trial, it is not a fair one.

7. The author makes fun of the king and queen, and he is merciless with the jury.

8. Don't go to Wonderland if you're looking for justice!

B. On the line, write whether the sentence is *complex* or *compound-complex*.

1. After Alice becomes small, she grows tall again. _____

2. Her height changes while she is in the courtroom. _____

3. She is so big that when she gets up she knocks over the jury box. _____

4. While she tries to put the creatures back in place, she apologizes. _____

5. Although she doesn't realize it at first, she puts Lizard back upside down, and then she has to turn him over. _____

6. Before she has said much, the king reads a new rule. _____

7. He wants to throw her out of court because she is more than a mile high, but she isn't really that tall. _____

APPOSITIVES AND APPOSITIVE PHRASES

> **RETEACHING:** An **appositive** is a noun or pronoun that appears beside another noun or pronoun and serves to explain or identify it. An **appositive phrase** is an appositive plus all its modifiers.

A. Complete each sentence below with an appositive that makes sense in the sentence.

1. One student, _____, got 60 signatures on the petition.

2. Another, _____, posted it in a nearby office building.

3. He was supported by his parents, _____.

4. The subject of the petition, _____, got a lot of attention.

5. An officially named group, _____, was formed to act.

B. Read the sentences below carefully. Rewrite each one, adding commas where they are needed.

1. Have you met Ms. Kerrigan the new naturalist at the Nature Center?

2. Their meeting with the naturalist was at the Owl House the largest building in the Nature Center.

3. Lynn the president of our group gave Ms. Kerrigan a copy of our concerns.

4. We knew that her reply a letter that was seven pages long would be a step in the right direction.

DIRECT QUOTATIONS

A. **Read the sentences below carefully. On the line indicate which are *indirect quotes* and which are *direct quotes*.**

1. Marty's father told him that he had to return Shiloh. _____

2. Marty said that he could not bear to part with the dog. _____

3. "I would do anything to keep Shiloh," Marty told his father. _____

4. "How are you going to prove that Judd mistreated the dog?" _____

5. "Just think about it," his father said. _____

6. "I have thought about it, that is all I can think about." _____

7. "I know it's a hard thing, son." _____

8. "I have to think of something," Marty said to himself. _____

9. "Dad, I need to talk to you about this." _____

B. **Read the sentences below. Underline the quoted words. If there is a speaker circle the speaker**

1. His mother said, "At least you have brought some joy into that dog's life."

2. His father told him, "It's Judd's dog and there is no way around it."

3. "I bet that Shiloh wants to stay with us."

4. "Shhhh, Shiloh," Marty whispered.

55

DIRECT QUOTATIONS

A. Insert commas, quotation marks, and periods where they are needed in the sentences below.

1. The weather today will be clear and sunny announced the weatherman.

2. That's good said my mother

3. It is always nice to have good weather for a picnic.

4. Get your stuff together children she called.

5. Where is that dog I asked

6. I think I saw him run under the bed in your room my sister said

7. Here Zeus I called

8. We might have to leave without him

9. There he is I said

B. Read each sentence carefully. Rewrite the indirect quotation as a direct quotation. Insert commas, quotation marks, and periods where they are needed.

1. The vet asked me if I had time to play with a puppy.

2. I answered that I would play with him every day after school.

3. My parents told her that the whole family will help take care of the puppy.

4. She asked me if I knew how important love and kindness were to a pet.

5. I insisted that I would never mistreat an animal.

COMMAS, COLONS, SEMICOLONS, AND PARENTHESES

A. Rewrite each part of the personal letter below, adding commas where they are needed.

1. March 22 2002 _____

2. Dear Melinda _____

3. I just finished a book about first ladies and I want to tell you about it.

   _____

4. It discussed Sarah Polk Eleanor Roosevelt and Hillary Clinton.

   _____

5. You can do an author search for it by typing in Peel Sherri.

   _____

6. It is fun interesting and easy to read.

   _____

7. Your friend _____

B. Add commas in each sentence where they are needed.

1. I looked up Eleanor Roosevelt in the encyclopedia and I discovered that her life was fascinating.

2. I read about Roosevelt's childhood her marriage and her life after Franklin's death.

3. Roosevelt was born on October 11 1884.

4. She was a mother a leader and a voice for democracy.

5. She died on November 7 1962.

COMMAS, COLONS, SEMICOLONS, AND PARENTHESES

A. **Rewrite each part of the business letter below, adding commas, semicolons, and colons where they are needed.**

1. September 7 2003 _____

2. Dear Ms. Murphy _____

3. I have scheduled our appointment for September 30 2003.

_____

4. Please plan to arrive at 300 P.M.

_____

5. We will discuss the following your contract your benefits and your new responsibilities.

_____

6. The meeting should last about thirty minutes however please allow extra time.

_____

7. Bring any questions you may have the meeting is a good opportunity to get them answered.

_____

8. Sincerely yours _____

B. **Insert commas, colons, and semicolons in each sentence where they are needed.**

1. Roosevelt had been a shy young woman therefore her leadership later in life surprised many people.

2. She traveled a great deal during her years as first lady she also wrote a newspaper column.

3. She traveled on her husband's behalf she said she was his "eyes and ears."

COMMAS, COLONS, SEMICOLONS, AND PARENTHESES

**Read the sentences below. Are the underlined words punctuated correctly?
Fill in the circle next to the right answer.**

1. We read about human rights, equal rights, and democracies.

   (a) rights equal rights, and

   (b) rights, equal rights and

   (c) correct as is

2. The United Nations was established on October 24 1945.

   (a) October, 24 1945

   (b) October 24, 1945

   (c) correct as is

3. It had many goals one was to save the world from war.

   (a) goals, one

   (b) goals; one

   (c) correct as is

4. Under the *League of Nations,* the index listed *Wilson Woodrow.*

   (a) *Wilson, Woodrow*

   (b) *, Wilson Woodrow*

   (c) correct as is

5. He helped form the League of Nations, however, it did not last.

   (a) Nations, however it

   (b) Nations; however, it

   (c) correct as is

6. The most important members of the United Nations include the following, the United States, France, and Great Britain.

   (a) following: the

   (b) following. The

   (c) correct as is

7. The United Nations was very important during the Cold War a time of great tension between the United States and the Soviet Union.

   (a) War (a time of great tension between the United States and the Soviet Union)

   (b) War. A time of great tension between the United States and the Soviet Union

   (c) correct as is

DIAGRAMMING SENTENCES

RETEACHING: **Diagramming** a sentence shows how all the words in a sentence work together.

A. In each sentence, underline the subject and circle the verb. Then diagram the sentence. The first one is already done.

subject	verb

1. Jenna spoke.

Jenna	spoke.

2. Legislators listened.

3. Rena stood up.

4. Mr. Duncan smiled.

B. Read each sentence. Underline the subject and circle the verb. Put an "X" over the direct object. Then diagram each sentence.

subject	verb	direct object

1. Rena climbed staircases.

2. Classmates rode buses.

3. Reporters took notes.

4. Legislators passed resolutions.

DIAGRAMMING SENTENCES

Diagram each sentence below.

1. The concerned citizens quickly wrote letters.

2. They were detailed letters.

3. Ann carefully explained the extremely complicated issue.

Page 4
A. 1. imperative 4. exclamatory
2. declarative 5. imperative
3. interrogative
B. 1. . 5. ? 9. ?
2. correct 6. correct 10. correct
3. ? 7. correct
4. correct 8. .

Page 5
A. 1. . declarative 6. . imperative
2. ? interrogative 7. ! exclamatory
3. ! exclamatory 8. . declarative
4. . declarative 9. . declarative
5. ? interrogative 10. ? interrogative
B. 1. c 2. b 3. a 4. d

Page 6
A. 1. a 2. b 3. c 4. a 5. c

B. 1. c 2. c 3. c 4. a 5. b

Page 7
A. 1. simple 5. simple
2. simple 6. simple
3. compound 7. compound
4. compound 8. compound
B. 1. Ms. Tory held Margaret's hand, but she did not speak.
2. Maizon kept Margaret from doing things, but now Maison is gone.
3. Margaret will try new things, or she will stay the same.
4. Margaret's dad died, and she lost her best friend.
5. The summer had brought sadness, and Margaret had suffered.
6. Next summer might be better, or it might be worse.
7. Margaret hoped for better times, but she couldn't count on them.

Page 8
1. Margaret's poem is long, but it is not complicated.
2. Margart does not discuss Maizon in this poem, but she does tell about her father's death.
3. The poem mentions Margaret's mother, and it quotes advice from Ms. Dell.
4. Margaret could have refused to write the poem, or (and) she could have refused to read it to the class.
5. The poem was well written, and Ms. Peazle was proud of Margaret's efforts.
6. The class did not say anything about the poem, but did they react to it?
7. Maybe no one knew what to say, or maybe the students were afraid to say the wrong thing.
8. The students were silent, but Ms. Peazle knew what to write.

Page 9
1. a 3. a 5. a 7. c 9. c
2. c 4. a 6. c 8. a 10. c

Page 10
A. 1. c 2. b 3. a
B. Possible answers:
1. She helped him discover the book.
2. Many books were found in the library.

3. It describes the things they saw.
4. His favorite tools are a hammer and saw.
C. 1. His first attempts were poetry. Ideas just came to him.
2. One example is a poem about Mexico. It was a short and funny one.
3. He read and wrote poems. A few years later he started writing short stories.
4. How did he create his characters? He just invented them.

Page 11
A. 1. fragment 3. correct 5. run on
2. fragment 4. run on
B. 1. Fresno, California, was the home of Gary Soto and his family.
2. He grew up using his imagination. This was how he became a writer.
3. It takes rest to have energy. Writing is difficult work.
4. He likes learning about language and words.
5. Life changed for Gary Soto when he went away to college. Suddenly everything was different.

Page 12
1. c 3. a 5. a 7. b 9. b
2. b 4. b 6. c 8. a 10. a

Page 13
1. The class read several articles about emergency medicine.
2. We read about workers who rescue very sick patients.
3. We learned that dispatchers make critical decisions when they answer a call.
4. A successful rescue requires the teamwork of different crews.
5. Some emergencies require both firefighters and paramedics.
B. 1. plural, plural, singular
2. plural, plural
3. plural, plural, plural, singular
4. plural, plural, singlular, singular
5. plural, singular, singular, plural

Page 14
A. 1. choppers, keys, days
2. nurses, boxes, infants
3. doctors, boys, spiders
4. medics, patches, trays
B. surgeons, helicopter, centers, lung, stretchers, backboard, babies, turkeys, family, classes

Page 15
1. c 3. a 5. c 7. b 9. b
2. c 4. b 6. b 8. a 10. a

Page 16
A. 1. Brian Robeson's adventure took place in Canada's wilderness.
2. The pilot's heart attack prevented Brian from reaching his father's house.
3. Brian thought his parents' television set would broadcast news of his disappearance.
4. The plane's cables formed a "birdcage" that almost trapped him underwater.
5. After one hard day's work, Brian's efforts paid off.

B. 1. forest's, singular possessive
2. problems', plural possessive
3. pack's, singular possessive
4. fuselage's singular possessive
5. boy's, singular possessive

Page 17
A. 1. Charles's
2. Photography Association's
3. Kendra Hawker's
4. video club's
5. newspaper's
6. photographers'
B. 1. painters' conference
2. Mrs. Raulerson's statements
3. boxes' contents
4. Venus's atmosphere
5. player's attitude
6. Mr. Roqmoore's presence

Page 18
1. a 3. b 5. c 7. b 9. c
2. c 4. b 6. b 8. c 10. a

Page 19
A. 1. William Butler Yeats, proper noun
2. The Lake Isle of Innisfree, proper noun
3. Irish, proper adjective
4. Yeats, Sligo, Ireland, proper nouns
5. Lough Gill Mountains, proper noun
6. Hazelwood Sculpture Trail, proper noun
B. America Irish
Armenian Poland
Taiwan Hawaiian

Page 20
1. Last Friday, Ms. Goldman's class went to the Museum of Science.
2. There is a beautiful building located at 525 Shelton Boulevard.
3. It was built sometime between World War II and the Korean War.
4. Is it next to the Thai restaurant called Siam Delight?
5. Is it across from the Midwood Professional Building?
6. Do we have to take Johnson Parkway to get there, Zach?
7. Will we pass by Greenleaf Associates where my Aunt Kim works?
8. At the museum, a Chinese-American scientist spoke to us.
9. Her name is Professor Amy Chow, and she is a friend of my uncle.
10. She grew up in Hong Kong and later moved to the United States of America.

Page 21
1. a 3. b 5. c 7. c 9. c
2. c 4. b 6. b 8. a 10. a

Page 22
A. 1. Road, Trail 4. Georgia
2. northeast, southwest 5. Missus
3. north, south, east, west 6. Avenue, Mountain
B. 1. Mr. , Mrs. 4. Dr. 7. Blvd., NE
2. Rte. 5. St.
3. Mtn. 6. Jr., Sr.

Page 23

A. 1. Dr. D. Chang
    2. Mr. B. White, Jr.
    3. 10 Thoreau Rd.
    4. Hanscom Blvd.
    5. Oak Ave.
    6. Troy, NY
    7. Moab, UT
    8. Fri., Jan. 4, 7 A.M.
    9. Connecticut St., SE
    10. PIN
    11. Mrs. M. Dyson
    12. Dr. C. Katz, Sr.
    13. Rte. 109
    14. Elm St.
    15. Mt. Royal
    16. Dayton, OH
    17. Boise, ID
    18. Mon., Aug. 9, 6 P.M.
    19. Massachusetts Ave., NW
    20. TV

Dr. Owen Russell, Sr.
Huntington Lakes Apts.
4432 Sunshine Blvd.
Del Ray Beach, FL 33446

Page 24

1. a   3. b   5. a   7. b   9. b
2. b   4. b   6. b   8. a   10. a

Page 25

A. 1. picks   3. grabs   5. knows
    2. looks   4. sees   6. makes
B. (possible answers)
    1. spotted   3. decided
    2. felt   4. wore

Page 26

A. 1. experiments 3. paste 5. pan
    2. samples   4. idea   6. question
B. (possible answers)
    1. bikes   3. a presentation
    2. a cake   4. the professor

Page 27

1. a   3. c   5. a   7. b   9. a
2. b   4. a   6. b   8. a   10. b

Page 28

A. 1. Most of the new flavors (tasted) delicious.
    2. Bubble gum (was) an unusual flavor.
    3. The ice cream (was) always fresh.
    4. Ice cream (is) a special treat for many people.
    5. Some flavors (became) famous.
    6. Others, like a garlic flavored one, (were) unsuccessful.
B. 1. predicate noun   5. predicate adjective
    2. linking verb   6. predicate noun
    3. predicate adjective 7. predicate adjective
    4. linking verb

Page 29

A. 1. Peppermint is a common (herb).
    2. Peppermint tea tastes (great).
    3. My peppermint shampoo smells (good) on my hair.
    4. For years, peppermint has been my favorite (plant).
    5. Even its name sounds (interesting)!
B. 1. Ben & Jerry's (is) a huge company in Vermont.
    2. Vermont (is) a beautiful state.
    3. In the fall, it (looks) especially dazzling.
    4. Nevertheless, the winters (seem) harsh.
    5. Vermont maple syrup (tastes) sweet.
    6. Its dairy products (seem) so fresh!

7. In the summer, the hillsides (appear) a rich, dark green.
8. For new beginnings, Vermont (has been) a favorite place.
9. It (has been) a popular skiing destination.
10. To me, Vermont (sounds) very attractive.

Page 30

1. a   3. a   5. c   7. b   9. a
2. c   4. b   6. b   8. b   10. b

Page 31

1. present   6. present   11. present
2. present   7. past   12. future
3. future   8. present   13. past
4. past   9. future   14. future
5. present   10. future   15. future

Page 32

1. looked   5. tried   9. supplies
2. shopped   6. will wear 10. will be
3. come   7. hemmed   11. carry
4. likes   8. change   12. will go

Page 33

1. a   3. b   5. c   7. a   9. b
2. c   4. c   6. c   8. a   10. a

Page 34

A. 1. grew   3. gave   5. told   7. did
    2. saw   4. said   6. became 8. lost
B. 1. grown   4. said   7. lost   10. written
    2. seen   5. told   8. thought
    3. given   6. become 9. made

Page 35

A. 1. became, become   7. made, made
    2. bought, bought   8. saw, seen
    3. broke, broken   9. sang, sung
    4. chose, chosen   10. spoke, spoken
    5. did, done   11. swam, swum
    6. gave, given   12. wrote, written
B. (Answers will vary.)

Page 36

A. 1. had done   5. will have tried
    2. had purchased   6. has been
    3. has been reading   7. had thought
    4. will have gained
B. 1. past perfect   6. present perfect
    2. present perfect   7. past perfect
    3. future perfect   8. present perfect
    4. present perfect   9. past perfect
    5. future perfect   10. future perfect

Page 37

A. 1. has earned   3. has helped
    2. has made   4. has given
B. 1. had asked   3. had spoken
    2. had thought   4. had said
C. 1. will have earned   4. will have met
    2. will have found   5. will have mowed
    3. will have learned

Page 38

A. 1. subject 3. object   5. object 7. subject
    2. object   4. subject 6. subject
B. 1. they   3. it   5. they   7. It
    2. them   4. It   6. us   8. They

Page 39

1. They   3. them   5. They   7. them
2. It   4. They   6. them

Page 40

1. a   3. a   5. b   7. a   9. b
2. a   4. b   6. b   8. b   10. a

Page 41

A. 1. his   4. our   7. our   10. his
    2. their 5. my   8. your
    3. their 6. their   9. my
B. 1. yours 3. hers   5. theirs 7. his
    2. mine   4. his   6. mine   8. yours

Page 42

A. 1. her   5. their   9. its   13. his
    2. our   6. Her, her 10. mine 14. ours
    3. Mine   7. Their   11. none   15. Mine
    4. her   8. My, his 12. her
B. 1. Mrs. Clark went to his first race.
    2. She saw that its trainer was standing ready.
    3. She was worried that his injury was painful.

Page 43

1. c   3. a   5. c   7. c   9. a
2. a   4. c   6. b   8. b   10. c

Page 44

A. 1. Many   5. Everyone   9. Few, anything
    2. Some   6. anyone   10. any
    3. All   7. everybody
    4. Several   8. Somebody
B. 1. indefinite   5. indefinite   9. not indefinite
    2. not indefinite 6. indefinite   10. indefinite
    3. indefinite   7. indefinite
    4. not indefinite 8. indefinite

Page 45

A. 1. Mary Cassatt   5. Edward Degas
    2. scenes   6. paintings
    3. painting   7. paintings
    4. Cassatt
B. 1. his or her   4. his or her   7. his or her
    2. their   5. his or her
    3. his or her   6. their

Page 46

1. c   3. c   5. a   7. c   9. c
2. a   4. a   6. a   8. a   10. b

Page 47

A. 1. show, shows   6. prefer, prefers
    2. learn, learns   7. need, needs
    3. touch, touches   8. miss, misses
    4. feel, feels   9. like, likes
    5. discuss, discusses   10. write, writes
B. 1. leaves   5. sing   9. watches
    2. whisper   6. bounces   10. dismisses
    3. sails   7. listen
    4. thinks   8. pass

Page 48

A. am, are, are, is
B. 1. do, does   2. have, has   3. go, goes
C. 1. has   3. are   5. am
    2. do   4. goes

Page 49

1. c   3. c   5. c   7. b   9. b
2. a   4. a   6. a   8. c   10. b

Page 50

1. Did you see (that) show at the National Postal Museum?
2. It is about the mail compartment on the Titanic.
3. It shows an old room with sea creatures growing in it.
4. (That) huge room contained thousands of letters.
5. The post office believes some of (these) letters could actually still be deliverable!
6. (This) interesting exhibit explains many problems related to the old mail.
7. First of all, (these) letters have been on the sea floor for about one hundred years.
8. Still, the post office must deliver all posted mail.
9. How will it find the relatives of (those) people?
10. What an expensive, difficult task it will be!
11. Still, could information in one of (those) letters change someone's life?
12. Could it solve a mystery or cure a broken heart?
13. Are valuable items in (those) decaying letters and packages?
14. Dealing with (this) mail will not be an easy task.
15. Yet, it does promise to be an exciting and fascinating one.

Page 51

1. Here, where
2. today, when
3. First, when
4. extremely, how
5. clearly, how
6. yesterday, when
7. Tragically, suddenly, totally; how,when, how
8. badly, how
9. here, now; where,when
10. sincerely, there; how, where
11. quickly, how
12. early, when
13. down, where

Page 52

A.
1. to the radio, adverb
2. by my side, adjective
3. at all hours, adverb
4. with headphones, adjective
5. in radio, adjective

B.
1. me
2. her
3. correct
4. correct
5. me
6. me

Page 53

A.
1. The white rabbit is an important character in this story.
2. The hatter is called a hatter because he makes hats.
3. When people use the word knave to talk about cards, they refer to a jack.
4. The word knave has other meanings, but it usually refers to "a sly person."
5. The knave is on trial although it seems clear that he did not commit a crime.
6. Although he has a trial, it is not a fair one.
7. The author makes fun of the king and queen, and he is merciless with the jury.
8. Don't go to Wonderland if you're looking for justice!

B.
1. complex
2. complex
3. coupound-complex
4. complex
5. compound-complex
6. complex
7. coupound-complex

Page 54

A. Possible answers:
1. out of our entire class
2. John
3. Mr. and Mrs. Petras
4. opening a skatepark
5. Skatepark Now

B.
1. Have you met Ms. Kerrigan, the new naturalist at the Nature Center?
2. Their meeting with the naturalist was at the Owl House, the largest building in the Nature Center.
3. Lynn, the president of our group, gave Ms. Kerrigan a copy of our concerns.
4. We knew that her reply, a letter that was seven pages long, would be a step in the right direction.

Page 55

A.
1. indirect
2. indirect
3. direct
4. direct
5. direct
6. direct
7. direct
8. direct
9. direct

B.
1. (His mother) said, "At least you have brought some joy into that dog's life."
2. (His father) told him, "It's Judd's dog and there is no way around it."
3. "I bet that Shiloh wants to stay with us."
4. "Shhh, Shiloh," (Marty) whispered.

Page 56

A.
1. "The weather today will be clear and sunny," announced the weatherman.
2. "That's good," said my mother.
3. "It is always nice to have good weather for a picnic."
4. "Get your stuff together, children," she called.
6. "Where is that dog?" I asked.
7. "Here, Zeus!" I called.
8. "We might have to leave with him."
9. "There he is," I said.

B.
1. The vet asked me, "Do you have time to play with a puppy?"
2. I answered, "I will play with him every day after school."
3. My parents said, "The whole family will help take care of the puppy."
4. She asked, "Do you know how important love and kindness are to a pet?"
5. "I would never mistreat an animal," I insisted.

Page 57

A.
1. March 22, 2002
2. Dear Melinda,
3. I just finished a book about first ladies, and I want to tell you about it.
4. It discussed Sarah Polk, Eleanor Roosevelt, and Hillary Clinton.
5. You can do an author search for it by typing in Peel, Sherri.
6. It is fun, interesting, and easy to read.
7. Your friend,

B.
1. I looked up Eleanor Roosevelt in the encyclopedia, and I discovered that her life was fascinating.
2. I read about Roosevelt's childhood, her marriage, and her life after Franklin's death.
3. Roosevelt was born on October 11, 1884.
4. She was a mother, a leader, and a voice for democracy.
5. She died on November 7, 1962.

Page 58

A.
1. September 7, 2003
2. Dear Ms. Murphy:
3. I have scheduled our appointment for September 30, 2003.
4. Please plan to arrive at 3:00 P.M.
5. We will discuss the following: your contract, your benefits, and your new responsibilities.
6. The meeting should last about thirty minutes; however, please allow extra time.
7. Bring any questions you may have; the meeting is a good opportunity to get them answered.
8. Sincerely yours,

B.
1. Roosevelt had been a shy young woman; therefore, her leadership later in life surprised many people.
2. She traveled a great deal during her years as first lady; she also wrote a newspaper column.
3. She traveled on her husband's behalf; she said she was his "eyes and ears."

Page 59

1. c
2. b
3. b
4. a
5. b
6. a
7. a

Page 60

A.

1.	legislators	listened
2.	Rena	stood up
3.	Mr. Duncan	smiled

B.

1.	Rena	climbed	staircases
2.	classmates	rode	buses
3.	reporters	took	notes
4.	legislators	passed	resolutions

Page 61

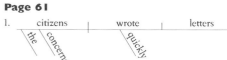

1. concerned citizens / the / wrote / quickly / letters
2. they / were / detailed / letters
3. Ann / explained / carefully / the / extremely / complicated / issue

Printed in Great Britain
by Amazon